★ POP CULTURE BIOS
SUPERSTARS

BELLA THORNE

SHAKING UP THE SMALL SCREEN

NADIA HIGGINS

L Lerner Publications Company
MINNEAPOLIS

Lerner Publications Company
A division of Lerner Publishing Group, Inc.
241 First Avenue North
Minneapolis, MN 55401 U.S.A.

Website address: www.lernerbooks.com

Library of Congress Cataloging-in-Publication Data

Higgins, Nadia.
    Bella Thorne : shaking up the small screen / by Nadia
Higgins.
        pages   cm. — (Pop culture bios: superstars)
    Includes index.
    ISBN 978-1-4677-1308-5 (lib. bdg. : alk. paper)
    ISBN 978-1-4677-1767-0 (eBook)
    1. Thorne, Bella, 1997-—Juvenile literature. 2. Actors—
United States—Biography—Juvenile literature. 3. Singers—
United States—Biography—Juvenile literature. I. Title.
PN2287.T46H55 2014
791.4502'8092—dc23 [B]   2013006917

Manufactured in the United States of America
1 – BP – 7/15/13

INTRODUCTION

Bella dolls up for a premiere in 2008.

It's 2006, and eight-year-old Bella Thorne has made a big decision. She wants to be an actor. Not someday—*now*.

It's not a crazy idea. She's been modeling since she was a baby. Her older brother is an actor. And yet, it *is* crazy, at least in Bella's mind. The third grader has dyslexia. How is she going to walk into an audition and read some random script? Read it cold and, even worse, out loud?

But Bella just isn't in the habit of dropping her dreams. Besides, she really wants this.

AUDITION =
a tryout for a role

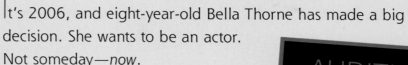

DYSLEXIA =
a condition that affects how the brain takes in letters and other information

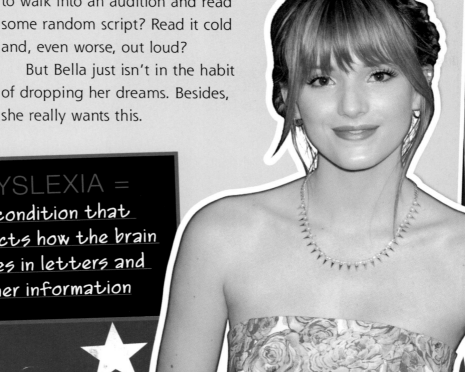

So one day, with a deep breath, she did it. She walked into her first audition. It was "THE worst," the teen actor recalls, laughing about it now. The casting people handed her a twenty-page script. They wanted her to talk to an imaginary dog. She just couldn't do it. Then she cried right in front of them! No surprise, she never got called back for the part.

Bella (LEFT) appears on a television show in 2008.

As an actor, Bella has experienced way more rejection than success. Still, she wouldn't trade her past for anything. **"I've worked so much harder at everything that I wanted to accomplish in life, and it just feels a lot better when I get there,"** she spilled to *HuffPost Teen*.

Needless to say, Bella moved on from that first audition in a big way. And her fans couldn't be happier for her!

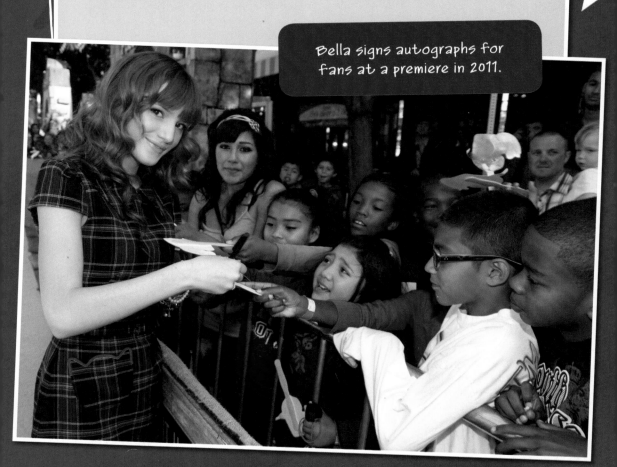

Bella signs autographs for fans at a premiere in 2011.

CHAPTER ONE

EARLY STRUGGLES

Bella Thorne says she's a lot like her character CeCe Jones on *Shake It Up*. They're both fireballs of energy. They're fashionistas, tomboys, rockers, and class clowns all at once.

Just try to find a photo of Bella without a smile. (It's hard!) But life's not all games and glitz for this Disney star. She has a huge heart, and her insane schedule includes tons of work for charity. And season 1 of Bella's own life had some pretty dramatic plotlines.

Bella stars as CeCe in the hit show *Shake It Up* on the Disney Channel.

Daddy's Cuban Princess

Annabella Avery Thorne was born October 8, 1997, in Pembroke Pines, Florida. She is the youngest of four, with two sisters, Dani and Kaili, and a brother, Remy.

Bella's father, Reinaldo, was Cuban, and Bella was born showing her Latin roots. The shape of her face just looks Cuban, she says. As a little kid, Bella spent a lot of time outside, and she was always tan in spite of her fair skin. She also ran around the house speaking Spanish—her first language. Her dad invented a special nickname just for her. She was his Cuban Princess.

BELLA BASICS

Height: 5 feet 4½ inches (1.6 m)
Pets: two dogs and three cats
Nicknames: Bells, Sassy B
Biggest addictions: texting and flossing
Girl crush: Jennifer Lawrence
BFF: Zendaya
BF: Tristan Klier
Causes: ending bullying, helping needy kids and animals

Bella brought her dog Kingston to a Halloween party in 2012.

Bella was still in diapers when she did her first photo shoot, for *Parents* magazine. She was a total natural in front of the camera, and the modeling jobs kept on coming.

Remy, Bella, Kaili, and Dani Thorne rock out at a red carpet event in 2008.

A Rude Awakening

Bells was a happy-go-lucky child. She felt safe in the love of her supertight family. So when she started kindergarten, she was shocked. Who knew kids could be so mean? Bullies called her weird because she spoke Spanish. Bella couldn't stand feeling different, so she dropped Spanish to fit in.

Then, in first grade, Bella got bullied again. When she would read in class, her brain mixed up letters or flipped them around. She couldn't make sense of the words. Bullies started calling her stupid, even though she's very bright. They shook her confidence so much that she still gets nervous when she has to read aloud.

In June 2012, Bella became a global ambassador for the organization Stomp Out Bullying! Here are her tips for ending the meanness.

1. Look inside. Are you a bully? Think about the words you use to speak to others.
2. See someone getting bullied? Stand up for him or her! Get an adult to help if needed.
3. Believe in yourself. Don't let a bully define who you are.

As it turned out, Bella had dyslexia. To improve her reading skills, Bella started reading everything in sight: menus, billboards, cereal boxes. It took about a year for Bella to catch up—but she did it. These days, she reads one level ahead of her grade.

Tragedy Strikes

In early 2006, the Thorne kids and their mother moved to Los Angeles to be closer to show biz. All four kids were models, and Remy's acting career was taking off. Inspired by her brother, Bella got up the nerve to start auditioning too.

DYSLEXIA 411

- People are born with it.
- It's hereditary (passed down from parents).
- It affects 15 to 20 percent of people in the United States.
- People with dyslexia usually have average or above-average intelligence.

In April 2007, nine-year-old Bella was super excited. Her dad would be joining the family again in less than one week! Then, just days before he was scheduled to arrive, a knock on the door shattered Bella's life. It was the police. Bella's father had died in a motorcycle accident.

For days, Bella couldn't cry. Then, finally, it sunk in—she would never see her father again. She freaked out and started screaming and crying.

After that, Bella started to heal. Her family was a huge part of that. Every year on Father's Day, the Thornes have a special way of remembering Reinaldo. They write messages to him on a balloon. Standing together in a circle, they read their words aloud. Then they release the balloon and watch it float into the sky.

FROM LEFT: Bella and her siblings Remy, Dani, and Kaili stand together in March 2007. They lost their dad the next month.

Bella (CENTER) attends a Disney press event in 2010.

CHAPTER TWO

A WORKING ACTOR

By 2008, Bella had been in more than forty TV commercials. She was constantly running from one audition to the next. Sometimes she'd have six callbacks for a single role. That cured her of her stage nerves!

Bells started getting small roles here and there. Finally, she won a steady part on *My Own Worst Enemy*...until it was canceled after just a few episodes. Still, the ten-year-old got to have superfun tickle fights with Taylor Lautner, who also had a role in *Enemy*.

CALLBACK = an audition for a part an actor has already tried out for

Bella (TOP) and Taylor played sister and brother on *My Own Worst Enemy*.

Bella got a bunch of roles playing the daughter on horror films and TV shows. Bella loved the work, but the films and shows were often too scary for kids to watch. She was bummed that her friends couldn't see her stuff.

Bella celebrated her thirteenth birthday with a big party in 2010.

Shake It Up

In early 2010, Bella landed an audition for *Shake It Up*. She didn't think the tryout went very well. She got tongue-tied in the middle and had to start over.

Bella had no real dance training. So how did she score a part on a show that was about dancing? Casting director Judy Taylor was wowed by Bells's personality.

"Bella is a total dynamo," Taylor said. "You want to get to know her better the instant you meet her."

Then there was the Z-factor—Bella's costar, Zendaya. The two girls had instant chemistry. During auditions, they improvised some moves together that were so tight that they almost seemed like a planned routine. Who could turn down such a sizzling duo?

**IMPROVISE =
to make up on the spot**

REAL-LIFE BESTIES

Bella probably spends more time with Zendaya than anyone else. They tape *Shake It Up* together. They perform live together. They travel together, *and* they Skype every night. "Even when I'm being annoying, I know Zendaya still loves me," Bella gushed to *Seventeen*.

The Hard Work Begins

After the *Shake It Up* pilot, Bella had six months before filming started again. She used that time to learn how to dance. Once again, Bella was up against her dyslexia, which causes some people, including Bella, to have a hard time telling left from right. Bella's solution? She took two to three dance classes four to five times a week. She fell so often that she had to wear knee and elbow pads. But by the end, Sassy B was keeping up with the pros.

PILOT = the first episode of a show that is used to sell the series to a network

SO EMBARRASSING!

One time, Bella was sitting next to Zendaya on a couch when Z spilled her water. No biggie, right? Bella helped her friend dry her wardrobe…but forgot about herself. She walked back on set with a wet bottom. Costume change, please!

Bella and Zendaya hang out while filming *Shake It Up* in 2012.

Bella, Zendaya, and the rest of the Shake It Up cast perform for a fan event in 2011.

Life on Set

Bella was used to being busy, but life got even crazier with *Shake It Up*. For Bella, each show wrapped in just one week. She got a script on Wednesday. By the next Tuesday, she was done with the taping.

A typical workday started at eight or earlier. Bella ate breakfast on set. She'd do schoolwork with a tutor and then work with her line coach. After lunch, she'd work with the rest of the cast. By late afternoon, she was running off to an interview or a charity event. She'd get back home a good twelve hours after she'd left. Whew!

LINE COACH =
a person who helps an
actor memorize lines

CHAPTER THREE

BRANCHING OUT

By early 2012, Bella had filmed dozens of *Shake It Up* episodes. The show was breaking all kinds of records. By season 2, it was the No. 1 TV show among U.S. kids. Bella loved that her fans were kids, like her. She called them her Bellarinas and Bellarinos.

Blogger, Performer

In February, Bella started a blog. Every day, she posts something new. Sure, she keeps fans up on her life. But the blog is also like a lifestyle magazine. She includes games, advice, fashion tips, and recipes. Every week, she highlights a charity and asks her fans to pitch in. Within a year, more than thirty thousand Bellarinas and Bellarinos had joined her site.

Bella and Zendaya give gifts to their fans in 2012.

Meanwhile, Bella's career as a vocalist was taking off. In March 2012, *Shake It Up: Live 2 Dance* came out. The sound track featured Bella's first single as a solo performer, "TTYLXOX." The fun song is a tribute to best friends everywhere. It went straight to No. 1 on Radio Disney.

In the summer, she and Zendaya released their funky hit, "Fashion Is My Kryptonite." And Bella teamed up with boy band IM5 for the dancy "Can't Stay Away." Now Bella's schedule included live music

SOUND TRACK = a recording of songs that go with a movie or a TV show

Bella performs with IM5 in 2012.

Every morning, Bella writes a line or two in her memory book about what she did the day before. Let's take a peek at what her diary might have looked like in August 2012.

Aug. 1: in NYC for interviews with Z

Aug. 12: took home "Best Young Actress in Television" at Imagen Awards! (RIGHT)

Aug. 17: "Shake It Up: Made in Japan" episode got record 4.54 mil viewers!

Aug. 24: off to fan meet and greet in CT

Aug. 31 (afternoon): delivered school supplies for kids in need

Aug. 31 (eve): live in concert with IM5!

performances. That gave her a case of major butterflies. But she pushed through and had a total blast.

In the fall, Bella started recording her own album. Bella says the album will feature all kinds of music, from dubstep to rock to hip-hop. **"My music is a lot like me,"** she spilled to *Teen Vogue*. **"[It's] a little weird and playful."**

DUBSTEP = a kind of dance music with a hard, electronic beat

Sweet Fifteen

Meanwhile, Bella was looking forward to a party she'd been planning for two years—her *quinceañera*. In Cuban culture, a girl's fifteenth birthday is as important as her wedding. For Bella, this bash would be a way to honor her father as well.

On October 22, 2012, Bella arrived at her party in a horse-drawn carriage. She had a full court of attendants, including Zendaya. She rocked a floor-length pink gown that she'd helped design herself.

Bella had asked her guests to bring canned food for a local food bank. Her menu featured all her favorite spicy Cuban dishes. After dinner, Bella shared a special dance with her sweetie, Tristan Klier.

Bella and her friends ride to her quinceañera in 2012.

Bella dances with her boyfriend, Tristan Klier, at her quinceañera.

Bella had met Tristan through a friend in 2011. Just a few weeks after the party, the adorable couple celebrated their first anniversary. Fifteen was shaping up to be a kickin' year for Sassy B!

BEST BF EVER?

Is Tristan the most romantic BF ever? Judge for yourself.

- He once brought Bella flowers he picked himself.
- He painted a surprise message on her mirror: "I love you and I'm glad I got to see you today."
- He often puts notes in her schoolbooks for her to find on set.

Teen Life and Beyond

These days, life continues to be awesome for Bella. She loves her job just as much as ever, and her friends help her stay grounded. On weekends, she often cheers on Tristan at his football games. She also enjoys visiting the humane society to pet and play with the animals there.

In addition, she gets manicures, goes bowling, watches movies, and serves food at soup kitchens.

SOUP KITCHEN = a place that serves hot meals to people in need

Tristan and Bella volunteer at a soup kitchen for Thanksgiving in 2012.

A lot of people have asked Bella where she sees herself in ten years. She's given lots of different answers. Expect twenty-something Bella to be either 1) a film star, 2) on a world tour, 3) designing her own clothes, or 4) heading her own charity. Of course, at the rate that Bella's going, it wouldn't come as a shock to anyone if she accomplishes all of this and more!

On her image: "I don't have to try to be perfect because I know my fans like me for who I am."
On being a role model: "I hope I can be the reason another little girl wants to be an actress."
On acting: "You have to believe in it all the way."

Bella gets a smooch from her BF, Tristan.

BELLA
PICS!

Zendaya, Remy, and Bella enjoy a night out in Los Angeles.

SOURCE NOTES

6   *Bella Thorne "I'm Answering Your Questions!"* YouTube video, 11:12, posted by Oceanmastergx, January 29, 2013, http://www.youtube.com/watch?v=HleATbvyvDA (March 28, 2013).

7   Anne Hilker, "Bella Thorne Talks Fame, Friends and 'Shake It Up,'" *HuffPost Teen*, August 21, 2012, http://www.huffingtonpost.com/anne-hilker/bella-thorne_b_1762029.html (February 13, 2013).

6   Justin Shady, "Bella Thorne," *Daily Variety*, October 22, 2010, A36.

17 Emily Laurence, "Bella Thorne's Relationship Secrets," *Seventeen*, n.d., http://www.seventeen .com/entertainment/features/bella-thorne-relationship-secrets#comments (February 13, 2013).

17 Sierra Tishgart, "Bella Thorne on Shake It Up and her Anti-Bullying Campaign," *Teen Vogue*, n.d., http://www.teenvogue.com/entertainment/tv/2012-08/bella-thorne-shake-it -up/?slide=4 (February 13, 2013).

25 Hilker, "Bella Thorne Talks Fame."

27 Ibid.

27 *Star Scoop*, "Bella Thorne Exclusive Interview," November 18, 2008, http://www .thestarscoop.com/interviews/bella-thorne-exclusive-interview/ (February 13, 2013).

27 "Bella Thorne—My Day, My Life," YouTube video, 4:00, posted by alloy, December 10, 2010, http://www.youtube.com/watch?v=BS_-bOgErJU (February 13, 2013).

MORE BELLA INFO

Bella Thorne Dyslexia Story
http://www.youtube.com/watch?v=4iVcTPRShBA
Bella won a Daytime Creative Emmy for this short video she made about her experience with dyslexia.

Bella Thorne's IMDb site
http://www.imdb.com/name/nm2254074
This is the best place to see a complete list of all Bella's roles in TV and film. It's long!

Bella Thorne's Official Site
http://bellathorneofficial.com
Yup, this is where you'll find Bella's awesome blog. If you sign up, Bells will send you e-mails every day.

Just Jared Jr.: Bella Thorne
http://www.justjaredjr.com/tags/bella-thorne
This celeb site for kids posts almost daily about what's up with Bella. You can tell the writers are total Bellarinas and Bellarinos!

Landau, Elaine. *Taylor Lautner: Twilight's Fearless Werewolf*. Minneapolis: Lerner Publications, 2013. Read about one of Bella's favorite (and most ticklish) costars.

Shake It Up: Disney Channel
http://disneychannel.disney.com/shake-it-up
This is the official site for *Shake It Up*. Start here for games, videos, and behind-the-scenes info on your favorite show.

INDEX

The images in this book are used with the permission of: © Kevin Mazur/WireImage/Getty Images, pp. 2, 27; © Michael Bezjian/WireImage/Getty Images, pp. 3 (top), 13, 24, 25; © Alberto E. Rodriguez/Getty Images for Staples, pp. 3 (bottom), 14 (bottom right); AP Photo/John Shearer/Invision, p. 4 (left); © S_bukley/ImageCollect, pp. 4 (right), 28 (right), 29 (top center); © Jeffrey Mayer/WireImage/Getty Images, p. 5; Danny Feld/© Touchstone Television/Courtesy: Everett Collection, p. 6; AP Photo/Alex J. Berliner/ABImages, p. 6; © Paul Redmond/FilmMagic/Getty Images, p. 8 (top); © Michael Buckner/Getty Images for mediaplacement, p. 8 (bottom left); © Gregg DeGuire/FilmMagic/Getty Images, p. 8 (bottom right); © Adam Larkey/Disney Channel via Getty Images, p. 9; © David Livingston/Getty Images, p. 10; © Dr. Billy Ingram/FilmMagic/Getty Images, p. 11; © Sbukley/Dreamstime.com, p. 14 (top); © Featureflash/Dreamstime.com, p. 14 (bottom right); © NBC/Getty Images, p. 15; © GTCRFOTO/ImageCollect, p. 16; Wagner Az/PacificCoastNews/Newscom, p. 17; BSA/ZOJ WENN Photos/Newscom, p. 18; Jen Lowery/Splash News/Newscom, p. 19; © Kevan Brooks/AdMedia/ImageCollect, p. 20 (top left); © Chelsea Lauren/WireImage/Getty Images, pp. 20 (top right), 22; © Paul Archuleta/FilmMagic/Getty Images, p. 20 (bottom); © Noel Vasquez/Getty Images for Extra, p. 21; © JC Olivera/WireImage/Getty Images, p. 23; © Albert L. Ortega/WireImage/Getty Images, p. 26; © Kevin Mazur/WireImage/Getty Images, p. 27; AP Photo/Todd Williamson/Invision, p. 28 (top left); © Byron Purvis/AdMedia/ImageCollect, pp. 28 (bottom left), 29 (top left, top right); Vincent Sandoval/BEImages/Rex USA, p. 29 (bottom).

Front Cover: © Carrie-nelson/ImageCollec (main); © S_bukley/ImageCollect (inset).
Back Cover: © S_bukley/ImageCollect.

Main body text set in Shannon Std Book 12/18.
Typeface provided by Monotype Typography.